HISTORY AT HOME

Rob David

ENGLISH HERITAGE

CONTENTS

English Heritage

RIGHT: Talking about the past at a museum.

ABOUT THIS BOOK

This book is written for parents and teachers in primary schools, who are interested in developing a home-school partnership in history. As well as providing examples of materials produced by parents and teachers to support family activities in the area of history, it also suggests a range of ideas which should help them to work together and develop children's skills in, and understanding of, history.

Most parents and teachers recognise that home and school have a shared role in developing children's reading skills. The role of parents in supporting other areas of the school curriculum is much less secure. On the one hand the government is encouraging home-school partnerships through the Parents' Charter, and on the other hand parents' organisations, such as the National Confederation of Parent-Teacher Associations, are seeking similar ends. If home-school partnership is to mean more than fund-raising and support for fieldwork, parents need to be given confidence in their own ability to contribute to their children's learning. This means helping them understand the aims of the school curriculum.

One of the subjects where parents can make a significant contribution is history. Many adults do not have fond memories of school history, and are conscious of their failure to remember dates and events and therefore do not see themselves as having anything to offer to their children which would support school history. Even though many younger parents have themselves been taught history with an emphasis on investigation, observation and deduction, the stereotype of history as a huge memory test of not very useful information persists. The supposition behind this book is that parents, particularly of younger children, can take a significant role in developing their children's understanding of history if the aims of the history curriculum are explained to them, alongside ideas for taking advantage of family occasions and activities.

The book focuses on four activities. Most families would find themselves able to do one or more of them in the normal course of events. It is based upon the experiences of a number of families and schools in Cumbria and includes support material jointly produced by parents and teachers. The core of the book introduces the four activities:

English Heritage

Looking at family photographs with an older relative.

- **In the family and at home**, which provides opportunities for historical investigation
- **Reading stories**, which helps to develop historical understanding and knowledge
- **Looking at buildings** and in particular the sometimes unspectacular ones common to most communities
- **Visiting museums and heritage centres** and knowing what to look at and what questions to ask.

In addition the book provides information on:

- the place of history skills and the content of the National Curriculum, in home-based activities
- making links between activities at home and school history
- cross-curricular learning opportunities through *History at Home*
- making a home-school partnership work
- books and other resources that would enhance the home-based contribution.

SCHOOL HISTORY AND HOME SUPPORT

History is a subject that ought to be well supported at home, whether by parents, the extended family, carers or family friends. However, many parents seem reluctant to become involved with their children's work in history, perhaps because of their own lack of confidence. This is partly the result of their own memories of school history and partly an uncertainty about the aims of history in the school curriculum.

The myth that history involves the regurgitation of vast quantities of easily forgotten historical facts persists, even though many of today's younger parents will themselves have been taught to analyze evidence, make observations and deduce outcomes. The lack of concentration on chronology and the rather random case studies used in history lessons during the 1970s and early 1980s have resulted in a generation of parents less secure about their knowledge of history, though more able to ask questions of evidence. When reminded, many parents remember above all else the case study of Tollund Man (the body in the bog) introduced to a whole generation of teenagers in Britain's secondary schools.

If home support is sought with historical content, then many parents will feel vulnerable because of their own lack of knowledge or incomplete memory.

Recommendations to visit sites or museums associated with study units may cause difficulties for many parents (especially if long distances have to be travelled and entrance fees are charged) and may not be convenient for families at the time the topic is being taught.

However, if parents are asked to help their children develop the skills associated with historical investigation, there are a number of clear advantages:

■ Activities can be carried out at the convenience of the family. As none of them need be linked to a particular study visit, the extra practice the children will get will benefit their general development of key historical skills.

Mike Corbishley

Interviewing relatives for their recollections can take place outside in the street where memories may be triggered by the changes that have taken place.

■ Activities can be suggested that use the resources available to many families in any locality.

■ No knowledge of historical events is needed by the parents. Questioning, investigating and discussing can be a family activity and can be fun.

■ If parents are shown how these activities benefit their children's schoolwork, they will have the satisfaction of knowing that they can support their children's education in a fairly painless way.

However, although most family activities need not be linked to particular study units in National Curriculum history, there are possibly two exceptions:

■ **Key Stage 1** children work on changes in their own lives and those of their family or adults around them. These children would benefit from parental support, and activities such as talking to relatives, looking at old photographs and reading some of the recommended story books, all of which would clearly enhance the children's school work.

■ **Key Stage 2** children work on a local study. These children might well benefit from home-based activities such as the ones associated with investigating buildings.

SUPPORTING HISTORICAL CONCEPTS AT HOME

There are two historical concepts which are especially easy to develop through family activities:

Sequence and chronology

Learning to put events in the right sequence allows children to develop a map of the past - a rather abstract map and therefore more difficult than the geographer's map of the world. Parents may not always be aware that the sequencing of events in a day, days in a week, months in a year, are crucial stepping stones for children's understanding of time. Most sequencing with young children may not seem like history at all. Equally, the vocabulary of time (eg new, old, before, after, now, in the old days) is a vital aspect of a young child's learning. Sequencing events in a child's own life and events in the life of a family develop from these starting points. Parents can support the school in developing a young child's understanding of time through normal everyday conversation.

As children get older, they need to become aware of longer time spans and particular events may need to be fitted into the correct sequence. This is where lack of confidence in remembering dates or the order in which periods of history took place, could worry parents. A way round this is to regard the solution to sequencing problems as a shared discovery in which all the family can take part. However, many of the 'events' which might be sequenced will be generated by the family activities in this book. Sequence and chronology may be investigated through:

■ dates when the buildings visited were constructed

■ the period in which stories that are read are set

■ the time at which various artefacts that are looked at were used.

Change and continuity

Some things change, others hardly change at all. Sometimes change is fast and continuous, at other times little happens for centuries. Thinking about why things change (or do not change) is fundamental to history. Practically all the suggested activities in the book will provide families with opportunities to look for change and discuss why it may have happened. For example change may be apparent in:

■ artefacts in museums and at home where changes in design and appearance will be apparent

■ buildings which have changed in use or in shape, eg windows and doors which have been blocked up or extensions which have been added

■ photographs which show changing fashions and hairstyles

■ stories, where change is part of the storyline, and may be a particular feature of the illustrations.

Activities at home which allow change to be noticed and encourage attempts at explanations will be a useful complement to work in school.

ESTABLISHING LINKS BETWEEN SCHOOL AND HOME

As the activities suggested in this book are not on the whole linked to specific study units, it is important that parents are helped to see the relevance of what they do at home. This can be done through an open evening at which the *History at Home* approach is launched (see page 30). However, schools will need to consider how they will keep parents informed of what is happening in history and how the skills and concepts learnt at home are also being developed in the classroom. It is important that parents are encouraged to keep returning to the project as opportunities arise. Schools might find it useful to:

■ display the titles of study units being taught in a place where parents will see them.

■ ensure that timelines are prominent features so that parents can see that their work on chronology is also being developed at school.

■ every so often choose a story to read from the list in this book (see page 34). When new stories are published draw parents' attention to them.

■ involve parents as people to be interviewed by the children for oral history and/or as assistants on visits to historic sites and museums. Such occasions form a type of in-service training for parents, especially when they are preceded by a joint planning session with the class teacher. This planning session is essential and will help them gain first-hand experience of the approaches which teachers take.

■ encourage children to talk to the rest of the class about what they have done at home. This could take the form of a book review, or a description of a place visited. Let children add home activities on to the class timeline.

■ establish a book borrowing scheme where parents can borrow copies of the recommended stories to read at home.

■ ask for family support in developing a school museum or a play area with a historical theme. As well as lending artefacts, parents could help with labelling and sorting and making props for the play area.

If parents see that the activities carried on at home have a bearing on what their child is learning at school, then the likelihood of the project continuing beyond the period of initial enthusiasm will be that much greater.

This hip bath in a museum sparked off an investigation about how bathtime has changed during the last 100 years.

English Heritage

TAKING ADVANTAGE OF HOME AND FAMILY

OUTSIDE YOUR HOME

Most families live in buildings that were built before their children were born, so the family home is as good a place to start as any. For those who live in very recently built homes, some of the ideas in the section *A day out with buildings* on page 15 may be more appropriate.

Homes are particularly effective at providing evidence of continuity and change. The opportunities are especially good if the home is part of an estate or terrace of similarly designed houses, because families will be able to compare their home with others that were once virtually identical.

Change is usually fairly easy to spot, and as there are always reasons for changes, it may be possible to work out why the change has taken place. Common changes include:

Adding extensions

As people expect more facilities, so extensions are added. Some of these additions may have taken place quite a long time ago. Many Victorian terraced houses did not have a separate kitchen space, any form of bathroom or an indoor toilet. Many houses of this type have extensions at the back and often the old outside toilet still exists as a shed at the bottom of the yard or garden. More recently it has become common to add an extra bedroom as families grow in size. Since the 1950s, and the availability of motor cars for the majority of people, garages have been added to houses which had been built without them. Porches, patio extensions, and more recently Victorian style conservatories are all examples of smaller extensions. They are often visible because of a change in the colour or size of brick, stone or rendering, and the use of slightly different roofing materials. Sometimes they become obvious when the house is compared with other similar ones in the area.

Rob David

These houses have had replacement windows and doors.

Replacing windows and front doors

This became particularly popular during the 1980s with the arrival of the large Do-It-Yourself warehouses. New style front doors, which tend to come in a limited range of designs, are easy to see particularly on older houses. Replacement windows need more careful looking for. Plastic ones, with glazing bars

English Heritage

A variety of chimney pots and aerials is easy to find.

that are stuck on to the glass are fairly obvious, but there are a lot of wooden ones which look like sash windows, until it is noticed that they open outwards rather than up or down.

Chimneys

Older houses often had several fireplaces and therefore a row of chimney pots on a large stack. Nowadays many of those chimney pots will either be capped or have been removed.

Aerials

Few houses built before the 1950s would have had television aerials,

MikeCorbishley

RIGHT: A garage extension with bedroom above.

and the 1980s saw the arrival of a new and very conspicuous addition to many houses - the satellite dish. Telephone wires will also be an addition to older buildings.

Change of use

Some people live in homes that began life as something else. In country areas the most obvious example is perhaps the barn conversion. In towns, redundant buildings such as mills, warehouses, chapels, schools and hospitals have often been turned into homes or new businesses. In these cases, the evidence of change is overwhelming especially if you can find a photograph of the building before it was converted.

Continuity

It is easy to begin to think that everything changes. It does not, and it is surprising how much continuity there is. It is sometimes less easy to spot but many homes still have their original features such as fireplaces, sometimes with their original surrounds, and chimney pots which are still in use. Picture rails, dados, tiling, stained glass are often still in place. In some houses, where items such as windows need replacing, the replacements are faithful copies of the originals.

Rob David

Changes to windows, door and boundary walls alter the original character of these houses.

English Heritage

In some older houses ornamental tiled floors survive, preserved as in this case by being covered by linoleum and later a carpet.

English Heritage

There is plenty of evidence that this house was formerly a corner shop.

Rob David

Satellite dish and relacement aluminium door both modernise this house and disfigure it.

English Heritage

ABOVE: Former chapel now in use as a tyre service outlet.

English Heritage

RIGHT: Another former chapel now used as a nightclub.

ARTEFACTS AND HEIRLOOMS

Many homes are miniature museums. Treasured items are handed down from generation to generation. Old fashioned gadgets find a second use, or if they have curiosity or aesthetic value, often find themselves on display. Family photograph albums are a treasure house of history. History really can begin with the home.

Artefacts

As a result of new technology and materials, and changing designs and fashion, most homes contain a mixture of recent and not so recent possessions. In the kitchen, plastic has replaced many items of wood, tin or enamel, some of which may still be in cupboards. Crockery designs change and commemorative cups and mugs are a particularly good source of history. Many Victorian and Edwardian items are now on display rather than used for their original purpose. Family heirlooms, by their very nature, will be from the past. Clothing fashions of the 1980s will be history for the young child, and some items lingering from the 1960s will be a source of amazement. Larger artefacts such as furniture may reveal changing materials and design. Such finds can stimulate discussion about why materials, designs and fashion change, and how changing technology has affected the way people live.

Photographs

One of the easiest and most enjoyable ways to help children understand change and relationships is through looking at photographs. Even photographs taken during the previous holiday introduce children to the past. The child will have his or her own history, which will be revealed through photographs:

■ Can children put photographs of themselves in the right order? Can they describe the changes that the photographs reveal?

■ Can they explain why those changes took place?

If photographs exist for other members of the family known to the children, hours of fun can be had looking at pictures of grown up relatives when they were younger. It might be possible to compare the articles of clothing worn by children at a number of different points in the last hundred years. A little more difficult, but equally rewarding, is to look at the different ways that the photographs have been taken and in particular the backgrounds. This links to changing technology and the ability to take 'snaps' rather than having to rely on studio portraits, with the consequence that people are seen wearing everyday clothes and performing a wide range of normal activities, rather than Sunday best in carefully selected poses. Cameras became cheaper and therefore more people could afford them and take their own pictures, and as a result what people recorded through photography changed.

English Heritage

ABOVE: Family collection of souvenirs.
BELOW & OPPOSITE: The family house is a treasure trove of artefacts from the past.

English Heritage

Does the photograph album reveal when sepia gave way to black and white, and black and white to colour pictures?

RELATIVES

An opportunity to talk with relatives or friends of the family should not be missed. It is an activity that will be enjoyed by young and old alike and will strengthen relationships. There is a wealth of fascination in changes in clothes, toys and games, and the school day. As well as changes, similarities will also occur. It is important that children appreciate that, in what appears to be a fast changing world, there are still many examples of continuity.

Conversations about 'what it used to be like' are valuable with people of any age. It is often thought that grandparents or great grandparents have most to offer because the changes that have taken place during their lifetimes are so conspicuous. However, it is surprising how much has changed during the shorter lifespan of parents, and conversations between parent and child will reveal a surprising degree of change and continuity over the more recent past.

There are a number of good topics of conversation:

- comparing childhood and games, past and present
- thinking about homes, their appearance and contents
- investigating changes in transport
- comparing holidays now and in the past.

It will probably be more effective if the family photograph collection is studied with the help of relatives. The realisation that granny or granddad was once a child comes as a surprise to young children. Elderly relatives will often be able to reveal more information about the family heirlooms and how the now disused artefacts that can be found in the home were used.

It will be useful to encourage families to complete their own family tree. You could photocopy the template provided on the following pages.

Mike Corbishley

ABOVE: Working on a family tree.
BELOW: Looking through photographs.

English Heritage

English Heritage

MY FAMILY TREE

Great Grandfather	
Name	
Born on	
Lived at	
Occupation	
Died on	Aged

Great Grandmother	
Name	
Born on	
Lived at	
Occupation	
Died on	Aged

Great Grandfather	
Name	
Born on	
Lived at	
Occupation	
Died on	Aged

Great Grandmother	
Name	
Born on	
Lived at	
Occupation	
Died on	Aged

Grandfather	
Name	
Born on	
Lived at	
Occupation	
Died on	Aged

Picture

Picture

Grandmother	
Name	
Born on	
Lived at	
Occupation	
Died on	Aged

My Father		
Name		
Born on	at	
He has	brothers and	sisters
Grew up in	Attended	school
Now lives at	His occupation is	
His hobbies are		

Picture

This is me		
Name		
Born on	at	sex
I have	brothers and	sisters
I live at	I attend	school
My hobbies are		
I hope to become a		

BY DATE

Great Grandfather

Name

Born on

Lived at

Occupation

Died on | Aged

Great Grandmother

Name

Born on

Lived at

Occupation

Died on | Aged

Great Grandfather

Name

Born on

Lived at

Occupation

Died on | Aged

Great Grandmother

Name

Born on

Lived at

Occupation

Died on | Aged

Grandfather

Name

Born on

Lived at

Occupation

Died on | Aged

Picture

Picture

Grandmother

Name

Born on

Lived at

Occupation

Died on | Aged

Picture

My Mother

Name

Born on at

She has brothers and sisters

Grew up in Attended school

Now lives at Her occupation is

Her hobbies are

My picture

BOOKS ABOUT HISTORY

READING STORIES

This is an area where many parents will be on familiar ground. The range of stories that can be read with young children is, of course, immense. Recently an increasing number of story books have been published which, in one way or another, can help to develop a child's historical understanding. Combining the skill of learning to read and a good historical story, is clearly an effective use of time. As well as story books, there are information books and these are considered on page 14. Different types of books are available for children of different ages:

■ Stories for younger children - picture books with limited text for children aged 4 - 8.

■ Stories for older children - children's fiction for competent readers of 8 and 9 years old and above.

Stories for younger children

The stories for younger children fall into a number of categories:

■ Stories that look at changes over a short time span - for example a week or a year. They are often designed as aids to help children learn the calender but are equally important to history where the idea of time passing is so fundamental.

■ Stories about families and everyday life are a valuable resource for introducing ideas of time and change. In these books, babies arrive, brothers and sisters grow older and grandparents tell tales of when they were young.

■ Stories that concentrate on time passing and the changes that take place. These can often be long periods of time and will therefore be more suitable for 7 year olds and above.

■ Stories about periods beyond living memory which offer information about different aspects of life in the past. Pictures and text introduce unfamiliar clothes, buildings, utensils, playthings and customs, suggesting the variety of ways in which people lived, worked and played in the past.

■ Stories involving people from other communities, such as Asian, African, Afro-Caribbean, Irish and Central European peoples.

■ Fairytales that are set in old buildings (eg castles) or involve people wearing clothes or taking part in activities from some past era.

Some good examples of books in each category are listed in the bibliography on page 34. Children's understanding will be enhanced if there is some discussion of the story and the pictures. To illustrate how this might be done, one story from each of the six categories has been selected, briefly described and some ideas for discussion suggested.

Our House on the Hill
by Philippe Dupasquier
A book that illustrates month by month a comfortable, happy, often familiar family life over the period of a year.

It might be useful to talk about the similarities in the day to day running of this family and that of the child, the weather through the seasons, farming through the seasons, social activities, such as festivals and birthdays, and how the family earns a living.

English Heritage

From Me to You
by Paul Rogers
A simple story told by Grandma linking an Edwardian childhood through the Second World War to the present day. A piece of lace features in many of the important events in Grandma's life - her christening, marriage and birth of her own daughter - and is used finally to edge a handkerchief which she gives to her granddaughter.

Note how each generation moves through the book, how the domestic scene is changing (gas lights to electricity). Ask questions such as:

■ How did people earn a living?

■ How were children punished?

■ What sort of jobs were women allowed to do compared with today?

■ Are any of the jobs the same?

The reader may wish to talk about the consequences of war; for example, the Grandfather in the story never came home. Talk about the old things you have. Ask older people questions about an old photograph, jewellery, a toy that they may still have. Another possibility is to talk about and make a keepsake that could be handed down to the next generation - a picture, a piece of sewing, for example, and talk about why families pass items on to subsequent generations.

Lost and Found
by Jill Paton Walsh
Four episodes in which a household item is lost by a child and found by a later generation. The pictures show the changes that take place in the domestic scene and the surrounding development from the individual house to the small village and market town and finally to the modern-day city.

Talk about the continuity that the lost objects provide and their links with the past. Think about why the children were asked to make the journeys. Compare the illustrations of the river and the settlements and talk about what is the same and what is different. Talk about what life might be like in each era.

■ What does the child think will happen next?

English Heritage

■ Who might find the scissors?

Clues in the Desert
by E Davis
This story, written in English and Urdu, tells the story of a Pakistani boy who returns to Pakistan to stay with his archaeologist aunt, and together they visit sites of the Indus Valley civilisation. The story reveals the terrific age and achievements in architecture, sculpture and technology of the Indus Valley civilisation over 4,000 years ago.

Talk about the differences in life in the Indus Valley civilisation and today, in both Britain and in modern Pakistan. What changes do they find? How do they interpret them?

Sir Cedric
by Roy Gerrard
A story told in rhyming verse of knights of old in which Sir Cedric rescues the Lady Matilda from Black Ned.

Look for the appearance of the buildings and the clothes people wore. What do the knights wear when fighting? Why do the horses look different?

Stories for older children

There is an enormous range of stories for older children. Some, which were possibly favourites of parents and grandparents, have become rather dated in their style of writing. For children between the ages of 7 and 11 it is possible to find and read stories associated with the periods of history they are studying at school. The main areas of study include:

■ The Ancient Greeks. The best books in this category are the retelling of the Greek myths.

■ Romans, Anglo-Saxons and Vikings. There are many more story books on the Vikings than on the other two civilisations. Myths and legends feature strongly, as do adventure stories.

■ The Tudor Period. A popular approach to telling stories about this period is the time warp, where present day children find themselves back in Tudor times. Some of the best stories are about Christopher Columbus, not strictly a Tudor personality, but making his famous voyages at the same time.

■ The Victorian Period. Stories tend to be written about children in factories and stately homes, thus introducing opportunities for social comment.

■ Britain Since 1930. Many of the stories from the recent past are set in the Second World War. Some are evacuee stories, others the adventures of children in blitzed cities. Some of the more interesting and difficult stories, which invite family discussion, introduce the harsher side of life in Europe during the war - refugees, concentration camps and being a Jew in Hitler's Germany.

Examples of books in each category are listed in the bibliography on page 34.

Stories involve the author in using his or her imagination to bring some events in the past alive. The balance that the author strikes between historical evidence and imagination is always interesting. Parents and teachers should ask whether the story sounds convincing. Does it conform to what you know about the period? There are opportunities here to check information given in stories with reference books - a useful exercise in historical enquiry for the children.

INFORMATION BOOKS

Many children have an insatiable appetite for information and there is an enormous range of books written for the 8 to 12 year old child which provide information about past civilizations. There are fewer books available for the younger child but in this age group children will acquire much of their information through the reading of stories. Your school library should have a good range of story and information books. Ask the School Library Service to provide a regular supply. It might also form the focus for displays at parents' evenings.

BELOW: Looking at books in the school library.

Choosing a book

With so many books to choose from, it is useful to have some criteria to help the purchaser make a good judgement. Don't choose a book just by its cover! It would be worth checking whether the book has :

■ a contents page and index to help the development of referencing skills

■ a glossary which explains unfamiliar words

■ pictures of real historical evidence such as artefacts, buildings and sites

■ artists' impressions of what places, objects and events might have been like

■ a text which not only provides information, but encourages children to think.

Mike Corbishley

A DAY OUT WITH BUILDINGS

Visiting ancient monuments, whether they are ruins or inhabited buildings, is a popular pastime for many families at weekends and during holidays. However, it often requires access to transport and can be expensive where admission charges are levied. Although there is no doubting the impact which many of our most famous ancient monuments can make, the emphasis on size, and artistic and historic significance, has tended to obscure the value of the more ordinary buildings in our own neighbourhoods. For younger children the scale and familiarity of local buildings makes their interpretation easier. In fact, because the neighbourhood is so familiar, it is often not really looked at, with the result that an investigation of local buildings will reveal features of interest for all the family.

The aim of an investigation of the neighbourhood should be to look for clues to the past. Some clues may be really obvious such as datestones and inscriptions, while others may be more subtle such as blocked up windows or doors which indicate change of use or plan. Some may permit interpretation then and there, others may encourage further questioning.

As examples we shall consider four buildings common to many communities. You will find activity sheets on each of these examples in the centre of the book which you may photocopy. Instructions on folding are given on page 18.

Our home

A number of ideas for looking at your own house were provided on page 6. Similar questions can be asked of other houses in your neighbourhood. In fact the activity becomes more interesting if it is possible to compare houses of

English Heritage

RIGHT: All of the examples shown here were found in one small town in the Lake District. From TOP LEFT CLOCKWISE: House with two date plaques; vernacular style of stone porch; former parish church now a house; former mill now a restaurant;former smithy now a fish and chip shop.

LEFT: Many chemist's shops still display traditional glass jars and bottles containing medicinal ingredients along with modern pre-packaged products.
ABOVE: Some shops still have cast iron frames to their windows, which often date from the nineteenth century.
BELOW LEFT: Exterior of grocer's shop with traditional displays both outside and inside.
BELOW RIGHT: Looking at a mural inside the parish church.

different types and different ages and to come to some judgement about who they were built for, and why.

A local shop

Nowadays, many shops are purpose built whether they are in town centres or out of town shopping malls. The local shop, whether it be the village store or the corner shop, often provides more interest as it may combine old features with new. If the shop has been established for a long time, elderly people can provide vivid descriptions of the furnishings and style of service of the past. Sometimes you might find buildings that have been converted into shops from something else, or shops that have become houses but still contain shop clues.

Looking at a gravestone in the graveyard of the parish church.

A parish church

The parish church is often one of the oldest buildings in the community and therefore reflects changes over a long period of time. The gravestones around the church provide fascinating information about the life and death of past inhabitants. Religious buildings of other faiths may sometimes be purpose built but are often converted from other buildings. Sometimes churches and chapels are no longer needed for their original purpose and take on a new use.

English Heritage

All the examples on this page are from the same small town in the Lake District as those on the previous page. It should not be difficult to find similar examples in almost any area of the country.

LEFT: Interior of grocers shop that still has many of the original fittings surviving and in use. Modern fittings which have been added respect the traditional fittings.

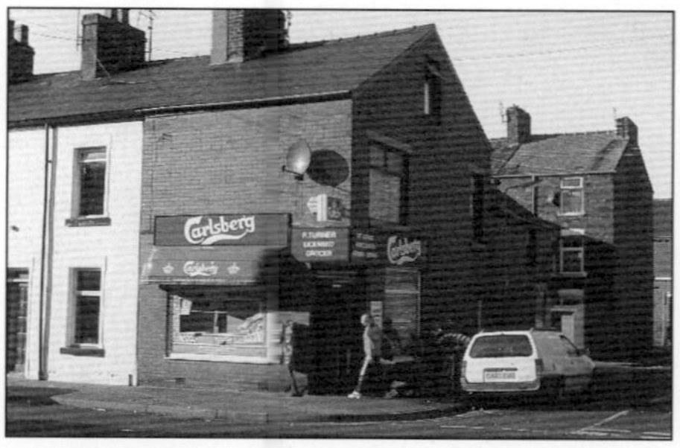

Traditional corner shop complete with modern fascia, blind and satellite dish.

ABOVE: Methodist Church built in 1899 as the Primitive Methodist Meeting Hall.

A railway station

One hundred years ago there were many more railway stations than there are today. Many redundant stations still survive as private homes, and goods yards and their associated buildings have been taken over by other industries. The evidence of their former use is often very clear. Stations that are still in use have had to be adapted to modern needs but many remain very much as they were. Most stations were built during the Victorian era and reflect the engineering and the craftsmanship of that period. They were often built to imitate other buildings, such as neighbouring castles and stately homes and used local building materials as well as more distant ones, such as slates and bricks, which the railways themselves were able to transport. There will be many railway clues around the station - sometimes they may be as small as initials of the original railway company on drainpipes and gate posts.

Rob David

TOP: Light and cast iron bracket at Ulverston station; the original light would have been powered by gas.

ABOVE: Detail of cast iron at Appleby station.

LEFT: Ulverston Station, Cumbria, ornate building in contrast to modern sign. The size of the station was more important in the past than it is today.

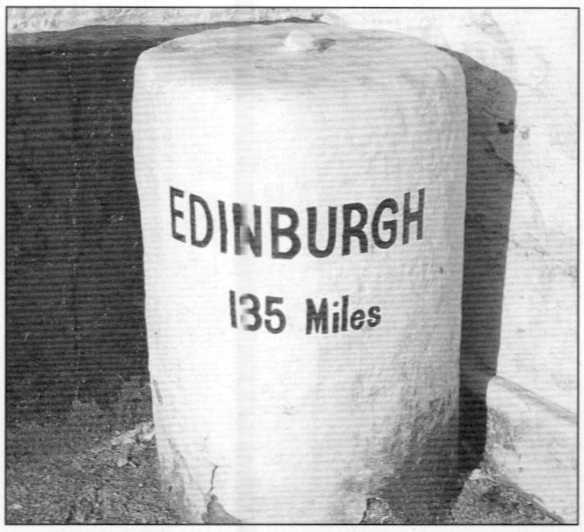

English Heritage

Rob David

LEFT: Milestones outside a coaching inn are a reminder of eighteenth and early nineteenth-century travel by coach and horses.

ABOVE: A Victorian country station imitating the design of other buildings found in small market towns.

Gillian Corbishley

Christopher Stell

English Heritage

LEFT: Some family snapshots from the past show not only how family members dressed but what their houses looked like at the time.

BELOW: A Detail from a tithe map of 1839 (for Great Oakley, Essex)

ABOVE LEFT: A Primitive Methodist chapel in Cumbria built in 1863. This photograph was taken in 1973 before its conversion into a house. ABOVE RIGHT: This photograph of 1991 shows how the building has been altered out of all recognition, although the plaque has been preserved as a reminder of the building's past.

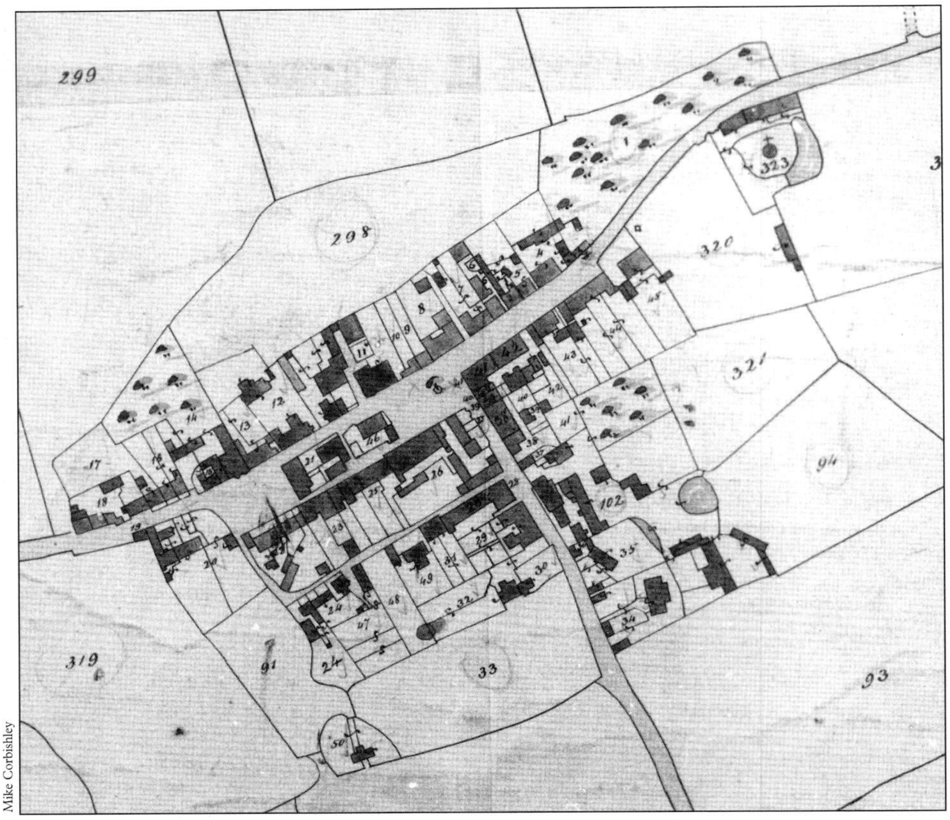

Mike Corbishley

HOW TO FIND OUT MORE

As the family investigates the buildings around them there will almost certainly be questions they cannot answer - questions such as, when was it built?, what did it look like?, what was its original use? There are ways of finding out the answers, although the older the building the harder it will often be:

■ Old photographs are often kept in the local library. Many books have been published recently which contain old photographs and postcards of a community.

■ Elderly people will often remember previous uses and appearances of buildings.

■ It is possible to find out the names and occupations of previous occupiers from documents such as the census enumerators returns (for the years 1841, 1851, 1861, 1871, 1881, 1891), electoral registers and from books such as Trade Directories. Libraries often have copies of these. If you live near a County Record Office, then they will often have them too.

■ Old maps can show when areas of towns and villages were built. If you find a very large scale map (25 inches or 50 inches to a mile) every building will be marked. Few maps that will be accurate enough will have been made before the end of the eighteenth century. Old maps are often kept in libraries and County Record Offices.

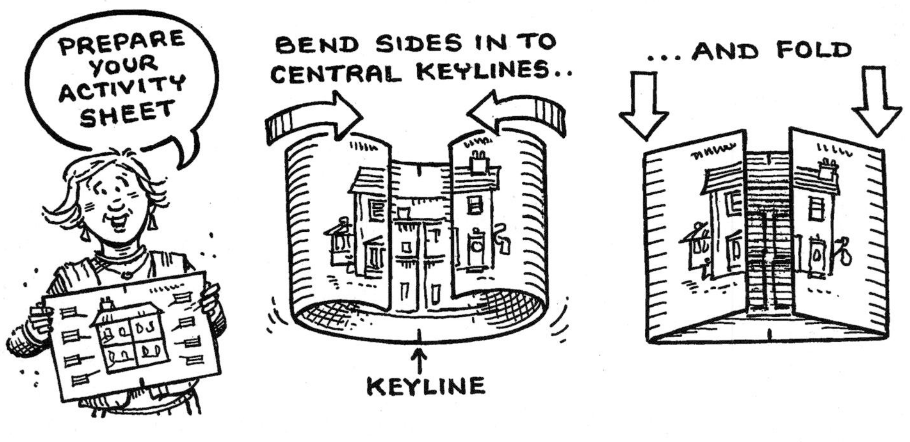

The photocopiable family activities enclosed in the centre of this book were originally drawn and designed as part of the *History at Home* project in Cumbria. You may photocopy them and fold them using the key lines.

OUTSIDE AND OTHER HOUSES OUR HOME

There is a surprising amountof history both outside and inside your home. Have a look at some of the things suggested in this sheet and see if it helps you to find out about the past.

WALLS
Is your home made of bricks, stone or something else? How thick are the walls? Can you find buildings with thicker walls? If you live near a castle or church go and look at their walls.

BINS
Every home throws out rubbish. How is yours collected? Is any of it such as paper, tins and bottles recycled? How was rubbish collected in the past?

DOORS
What do you notice about front doors? Are they all the same size? If you can, look at some on older buildings. Why have some doors got a porch?

YOUR HOME
Is your house terraced, detached or semi-detached? Or is it a flat? What sort of building is it?

ROOFS
Generally the steeper the pitch of the roof, the older the building. A roof keeps the water out of your home. Look at some roofs near you. Can you see the differences? Which do you think is the oldest/youngest? What are they made of? Where does the rain go?

Outside your house you many have a balcony, back-yard or a garden, and sometimes outbuildings such as a garage or shed. Can you find older ones such as a toilet or coal-shed?

CHIMNEYS
Some modern homes don't have a chimney. Why? What are chimneys for? Look at some older buildings in your town or village. Can you draw their chimneys? Find a very big chimney. Can you estimate how tall it is?

1900 | 1910 | 1920 | 1930 | 1940 | 1950 | 1960 | 1970 | 1980 | 1990

Can you put the birth dates of any members of your family on this time line? Does your house fit on? How about other buildings you know?

WINDOWS
Have you ever looked at windows? How many different sorts can you see? Really old buildings might just have slits. Can you think of a reason for this? Have you seen a building with a whole wall of glass? Do you think it is old or modern?

ALTERATIONS
Is there any evidence that your house has been altered? Look for blocked-up windows or doors, patches of different building materials and extensions.

INSIDE

We have specialist rooms. A very long time ago more happened in less space. Kitchens were in a separate building. People lived, slept and bathed in the same room.

THE BATHROOM
Have bathrooms always been like ours? Is there someone you can ask? Toilets have not always been inside the house, nor have they flushed. Can you ask someone about this? How does the water get into the bathroom? Do you use more water for a bath or shower? Is there a way to find out?

THE SITTING ROOM
What do you do in your sitting room? Is this different from what happened when your grandparents were children? Before central heating, open fires were more important as they were our only means of keeping warm. Can you ask anyone what it was like? Fires and chimneys have got smaller and modern fuel is more efficient. Old chimneys are quite interesting. Can you find out anything about them?

ARTEFACTS
Look around your home, or grandparents'. Can you see anything that might have been used in her home years ago? For instance, for ironing, washing, cooking or heating?

STAIRS
All buildings with two storeys need some sort of staircase. Over the years these have progressed from ladders to wooden copnstructions depending on age, cost and space.

KEEPING WARM
How do we keep warm? See if you can find out how people kept warm before central heating or electric blankets.

CURTAINS
We use curtains to be private and as part of our decor. That has not always been so. Why were they used in the past? What else was used instead of, or as well as curtains?

WASHING AND COOKING
How does mum do the washing? Did your grandmother's mum do it this way? Find out how it was done. Where does the water from the sink go?

Has it always been like this? Did your grandparents use electricity or gas or something else to cook with? They may have lived far away from here, even in another country where things were very different. What do we have that they didn't have?

FLOORS
The earliest floors were hard earth covered with rushes. Over the years stone flags, tiles, linoleum, polished wood, rugs and carpets have been used. Today you might see a variety of these because people can choose what suits them best.

SHOP

Shops and shopping are constantly changing. What happened only 20 years ago is different from today. All grown-ups can tell you something of what shopping was like for them as children.

WINDOW SHOPPING
What is displayed in the window? Can you tell what the shop sells? Are you tempted to go in? Do you think displays always looked like this? Is there someone you know who could talk to you about what displays used to be like?

AROUND THE SHOP

Can you walk to your shop?

A shop can be a centre for the community, where people meet and exchange news and gossip.

Street names are interesting. Are there any strange ones near you?

What are the buildings on each side like?

You may have different kinds of local shops. How many are there in your area and what do they sell?

SIGNS
How many different signs are there outside the shop? Some shops have very unusual signs? You might spend some time looking for them in the street and finding out what they mean.

This activity was devised as part of the History at Home project. It has been re-drawn by Dai Owen. c English Heritage 1996.

A LOCAL

Can you tell by looking at the shop when it was built?

What materials were used to build the shop?

WINDOWS
Look at the windows. Windows of shops are often different from house windows. The size, signs, stained glass or etching might tell you about the history of the shop.

INSIDE OUR SHOP

What is your first impression when you go in? Is it light or dark? Welcoming? Are there any nice or unusual smells? Can you reach the top shelf? How are the goods displayed?

Some people find it difficult to get in and go around the shop. Could someone in a wheelchair use your shop?

Why did shops have a chair?

Do you help yourself or are you served? Do you think it has always been like this?

How are goods packaged on the shelves?
Is so much packaging necessary?
Were goods packaged like this when your grandparents were children?

Why are goods arranged the way they are?
Where have they all come from?
Was there always this choice?

STAFF
How many assistants are there?

What are they doing?

UNIFORMS
Are the assistants wearing uniforms?
Were uniforms worn in the past?

THE WAY WE PAY
How does mum or dad pay? They might use a cheque, a plastic card or cash. Has this always been the same?

THE TILL
You are probably used to queuing at the till. Many goods are processed with a bar code or label. The till does all the adding up. Not long ago this was quite different. Ask about it.

How are goods packed for you to take away?

Can items be weighed in your shop or is it all pre-packed? This is something else you could talk to an older person about.

FROZEN FOOD
Most families have a fridge/freezer these days. This means the we don't have to shop every day. When your grandparents were young this was not the case.
Talk to them about it.

FIND OUT WHAT HAPPENED TO OUR MONEY IN 1971.

CHURCH

DETAILS AND CLUES TO LOOK FOR

THE PARISH

What do you think it is made from? Brick or stone? Or something else?

What shape are the windows? Are there any clues which show that the church was built at different times? You could look for blocked-up windows and doors, different styles of windows, different types and age of building material, straight line joints.

Is the church on a hill, or is it in the middle of lots of shops or houses? Does it stand out from the buildings around it?

The lychgate marks the entrance to the churchyard.

WINDOW STYLES
The shape of church windows changed over centuries, and gives a good indication of date.

Norman c.1100AD · Early English c 1200AD · Decorated c.1300AD · Perpendicular c.1400AD

Where a new wall has been added to an old one you can often see the join as a STRAIGHT LINE JOINT.

ROOD SCREEN
separated the clergy in the chancel from the congregation in the nave. Rood means the Cross.

TRIPLE DECKER PULPIT
The parish clerk sat in the lower deck, while the parson read the service from the middle deck, but preached from the top deck.

A CARVED ANGEL used to decorate a roof. They were richly coloured.

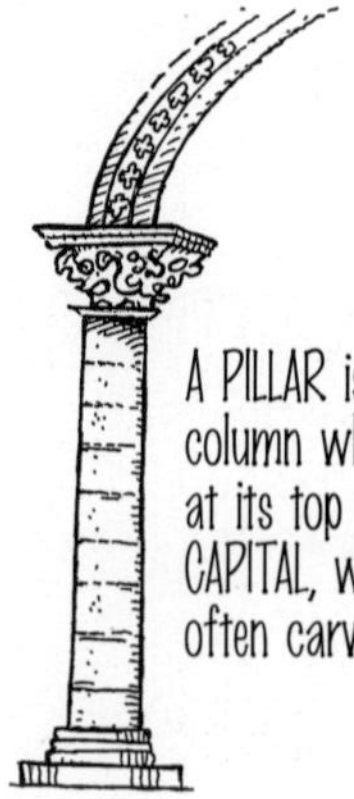

A PILLAR is a column which has at its top a CAPITAL, which is often carved.

BOX PEWS
were originally paid for by the richer members of the parish. In the eighteenth century they became popular for all members of the congregation. They helped keep out the draughts.

Is there a church near you? Does it look new or old? Is it tall with a high tower like this one or does it have a spire?

Does it have a clock like this one?

Does it have a churchyard with gravestones? Are these all the same shape or not? What is the oldest date you can find on a gravestone? Do the styles of gravestones change?

Yew trees have often grown in graveyards for centuries.

THINGS TO LOOK FOR INSIDE

A church is used for Christian worship. Do you see this symbol anywhere?

As you walk inside a church, what do you notice first? Is it very quiet and still, or are there lots of people around, the sound of traffic outside?

THE ARCHES
Have a look at the arches. Round headed arches are usually older than pointed ones. What shapes are the pillars? Are the capitals plain or decorated?

MUSIC
When people sing in this church, do they have an organ or a piano to help them?

GLASS
Are the windows full of clear glass or stained glass? Can you tell whether the stained glass is very modern or Victorian? Occasionally some medieval glass survives.

THE PULPIT
What is it made from? Sometimes triple decker pulpits survive.

THE ROOF
In very big churches you may find a stone vault, but most churches have a wooden roof. Some old roofs are beautifully decorated with angels and coats of arms.

MEMORIALS
There may be some writing on walls of the church. What is it about? Are there different kinds of memorials? Do you recognize any of the local names? Sometimes important people were buried inside the church in carved tombs.

THE BELLS
The bells are rung to summon people to services. Can you see where they are hung? How are they rung?

THE ALTAR
All the seats in church face the same way. As you sit down you will be facing a table, altar, or holy table. Can you find out what it is used for? If it's covered does it have a special colour? What is on it? The altar is up a step in the CHANCEL in the wall by the altar you will sometimes see a recess for the holy water stoop and a small cupboard called an aumbrey.

When people read the Bible in church, is there a special place to read it from? There might be an eagle carved into the stand or lectern. The eagle is a symbol of the resurrection and ascension of Jesus.

CHRISTENING
Is there a font for children to be christened?

PARISH CHEST
Is there an old wooden chest in the church? This is the Parish Chest in which documents used to be kept. It usually had three locks. The vicar and churchwardens each kept a key and they all had to be present to open the chest. Why do you think there were three keys?

SEATS
Where are people meant to sit? Are there wooden pews, or individual chairs? The seats are usually in the NAVE. Some churches still have very old pews with doors, known as box pews.

STATION

Towards the end of the 19th century most towns and villages were linked by railways. How do you think your station helped to develop your town?

The company which built the station wanted it to look good. This might have included a spacious covered roof, decorative railings, flower beds and patterns or designs. What can you find on your station which makes it attractive? What designs and patterns can you find?

GOODS AND SIDINGS

In order to allow passenger trains through the railway station, goods were loaded and unloaded in a siding which was a branch off the main line. Can you see a siding at your station? Is there a goods shed? What is it used for now?

Are there any factories or warehouses near your station? Many companies used the railway for transporting goods.

One of the most important goods that would have been carried was COAL. Can you see any evidence at your station of this? What else might have been carried on these goods trains?

The signal box controls the signals on the line. The older ones were often made of wood and dooorated.

Old Ordnance Survey maps will show where abandoned lines once ran.

A RAILWAY

As you approached the station did you notice a symbol for the station?

Is your railway station in the centre or on the outskirts of your village or town? How do you get to the station?

Once there were many different railway companies. One was London Midland Scottish. Can you find any evidence which shows the company your station once belonged to?

After this all companies united and became British Railways, but now there are many different companies again. Which company uses your station?

PLATFORMS AND PASSENGERS

Your railway station could be a main line station or on a branch line. Perhaps it is used at certain times more than others. How can you tell? Can people travel in different directions?

Where can you obtain a ticket? It might be a ticket office, a machine or on the train. Is the ticket office at your station still used? Does the booking clerk use a computer? Older people will be able to tell you what tickets used to be like.

Your station could be a modern design or perhaps it is much older. If it is old perhaps it was made from the same stone as local buildings. Can you find anything to tell you how old the station is?

Stations often have lots of chimneys. Which rooms have fireplaces? Are any of them still used?

Different stations have different ways of telling you about train departures and arrivals. How can you find out this information at your station?

An essential part of a railway station has always been a clock. Can you see your station clock? Do you think it has been there a long time?

Do you know anyone who travels on trains?

In the past most stations would have provided a General Waiting Room and a Ladies Room. There were reasons why there was a Ladies Room. Can you suggest any?

How do you get from one platform to another?

In the past stations often had a station master who lived in a house on the platform (or nearby), a booking clerk, porters (who carried luggage) and cleaners. Most stations would have their own signal box and signalmen. How many people work there today?

Is there anywhere you can buy food and drink on your station? At larger railway stations there may be a buffet. In the past passengers may have bought refreshments which were available from a trolley on the platform. What has replaced the trolley today?

The railway workers who worked for a particular company were very loyal. They wore their own company's uniform with great pride. What is the uniform like today? Look out for the railway symbol.

VISITING MUSEUMS AND HERITAGE CENTRES

There is an extraordinary variety of museums in Britain, and the majority in one way or another contain 'historical' collections. For many families there will be a museum nearby. So many museums have changed their approach to displays in recent years, that parents who have not paid a visit recently, may well be surprised at what they find.

MUSEUMS

Very often it is the natural history rather than the historical collections in museums which enthuse young children. It is easier to place the stuffed animals into some form of context, however inaccurate, than it is the historical artefact. What is missing from many historical displays is any help in understanding the people who used the old artefacts. Where the human element is incorporated as at the big open air museums at Beamish and Ironbridge Gorge, or contexts are provided such as the reconstruction of part of Viking York at Jorvik, children's involvement is assured. The challenge facing parents at the majority of museums is helping their children consider the artefacts that they are looking at as made and used by people. When an interesting display has been located, the family need to try and answer a range of questions about the artefacts. Questions will vary from display to display but will probably include some of the following:

- What is it made from?
- How old is it?
- What was it used for?
- Have we seen something like it before?
- Who might have used it?

The Canterbury Tales Visitor Attraction

The Canterbury Tales Visitor Attraction

English Heritage

TOP & CENTRE: Visiting the Canterbury Tales.
BOTTOM: Local museums have collections that reflect the locality. Many have reconstructions of shops and workshops.

- Why is it in the museum?
- Is it valuable?
- How can we find out more?

Families should be encouraged to avoid the temptation to try to see too much - a severe temptation in all big museums. A well planned visit where the family decide what type of exhibits they wish to see will result in a more enjoyable time for all.

HERITAGE CENTRES

Heritage centres are becoming more common and more popular. They are having an enormous impact on how we see the past. While museums often try to let us make up our own mind about what the past was like, by looking at the artefacts that remain from the past, heritage centres tend to tell us what the past was like, or what the designer wants us to think the past was like. Many heritage centres do not contain anything original at all - buildings are re-created and the scenes within them contain only replicas. It is very easy to be seduced by the heritage centre unless the visitor comes with either an open mind, or background knowledge, or both.

For families, visiting a heritage centre can be an extremely enjoyable activity and can enthuse children with an interest in the past. However, parents might like to have two questions in the back of their minds, perhaps to talk about when travelling home at the end of the day:

- What did we see that was real?
- Was the past really like what we saw?

Through asking these sorts of questions parents will begin to help their children understand that what they have seen is an interpretation of the past and that interpretations are just that.

MAKING A HOME-SCHOOL PARTNERSHIP WORK

Moving Home-School partnerships from fund-raising and social events into the curriculum is difficult and the benefits long term. No one would expect over-night improvements in reading skills, and progress in other areas will be even slower because the opportunities will be less frequent.

If a partnership to develop children's understanding of history is to have any chance of success, then the following conditions have to be right:

- it must be a genuine partnership - parents have to be really working alongside the teachers.

- parents must be confident that they understand what they are doing and why they are doing it and that the activities can be carried out with a minimum of effort and in the families' own time, and can be shown to be fun.

- the school can show parents, reasonably consistently, that there are real links between the home-based activities and the children's learning in school.

A GENUINE PARTNERSHIP

All the materials that have been printed in this book were created by small teams of parents and teachers, in equal numbers. When asking for parental support, schools requested that parents who were otherwise teachers, and parents with a professional interest in history, did not volunteer. It is important that, as far as possible, the parents who are involved in the creation of materials are seen by their peers as being similar to themselves. It is important that parents are saying to each other 'if they can do it, so can we'.

Even if parents and teachers decide to use some or all of the materials that are printed in this book, it would be a very good idea to organise some teams of parents and teachers to design some additional ones. For example, the activity sheets have been written to be applicable to most buildings in a particular category. The area of the school community may contain one or two buildings of special interest and similar leaflets could be produced for them. Other possibilities include making a museum-specific booklet for a local museum or heritage centre and to write further 'questions to ask' sheets for other story books on the list on page 34.

These volunteer parents will almost certainly enjoy what they are doing, because their close involvement will mean that they quickly understand what history is aiming at and therefore why they are doing it. These parents will be particularly valuable when the time comes to widen the partnership to as many families as possible. The most effective way is an open evening when the parents are invited to a display of history by their children involving as many forms of presentation as possible. What the parents see will complement the accompanying presentation of the home-based history materials. Parents will be able to see what their children are doing and how they are doing it and recognise that the home activities are clearly developing the same skills. If the parents, rather than the teachers, present the home activity materials, parental confidence that they too can do it will be massively enhanced.

PARENTAL CONFIDENCE

The biggest challenge is to capture interest and communicate enthusiasm. Obviously, it will never be

Mike Corbishley

Family featured in *History at Home* video working on their family tree project.

possible to make everyone interested but there are a number of strategies which will help to increase confidence and as a result enhance interest.

■ Show that all the activities involve families investigating together - that it is the questioning and deducing that is important, and that detailed historical knowledge is not required, although many adults will be surprised how much general knowledge they have which will be relevant.

■ Ask for help from parents and grandparents in loaning old artefacts and photographs and talking with the children about the past. The more parents see what their children are doing in class and the approaches adopted by the teacher, the more they will appreciate the contribution they can make and the relevance of the *History at Home* material.

■ Let parents encourage parents but ensure there is a strong point of contact with the school, possibly through the curriculum co-ordinator for history, who can provide reassurance and encouragement. If a story-book loan scheme operates, 'exchange' day could promote discussion.

■ Emphasise opportunities for developing reading and writing skills through *History at Home* activities.

■ Point out that *History at Home* activities will promote such useful lifeskills as listening to others, keeping an open mind, having an opinion and supporting a point of view.

A MINIMUM OF EFFORT

Everyone is busy and families have their own priorities. It is not helpful to link these home activities to particular parts of the programme of study of the National Curriculum and as a result require them to be done during a certain part of a term. All the activities are free of specific content and are designed to develop skills alongside work carried out in school. In effect, the activities provide children with more practice and in some ways

Mike Corbishley

Looking at a flat iron - scene from *History at Home* video.

would be ideally positioned when history was not a focus of the school curriculum as they will provide further practice at a range of skills. When introducing the materials to parents,

■ Stress that there is no time limit and activities can be used again and again, as children will always gain something new from them.

■ Emphasize that children will be learning and practising all the skills in normal classwork, so if a family is unable to do all the activities, their children will not be missing out on any aspect of history. The activities provide further practice, not the only practice, at particular types of investigation.

■ Make it clear that there is no need to do all the activities. Any of the activities will help their children. In many ways, the story activity is easiest because most parents are reading stories anyway. Other families have become enthusiastic about the family tree activities with the whole family, of all generations, becoming involved. Looking at buildings or visiting museums will often have to wait for holidays but for many families a visit to a castle or a heritage centre is a feature of a summer holiday. However, as most families are surrounded by buildings, which do not require long journeys or have entrance charges, confidence will be developed if it is stressed that these activities can take place at almost any building.

■ Show the English Heritage video '*History at Home*'. This shows how the investigations can take place as part of normal family activities. It also shows that everybody can enjoy what they are doing.

REAL CURRICULUM LINKS

Families that take on the *History at Home* material will be investing time, effort (and sometimes money) in the activities. It is, therefore, very important that parents can see that what they are doing will enhance their children's performance in and enjoyment of history. This can best be achieved by:

■ Showing parents, through displays and activities at a parents evening, what school history is aiming at. It will then become self evident that the *History at Home* materials are aiming at the same sort of thing.

■ Keeping parents informed of history activities in school, thus showing that the same skills are being taught, though possibly in different historical contexts.

■ Providing opportunities for children to contribute their *History at Home* discussions to class discussions and displays.

The *History at Home* video is a good introduction to investigating both family and local history, presented in an accessible way.

A TIMETABLE FOR SETTING UP HISTORY AT HOME

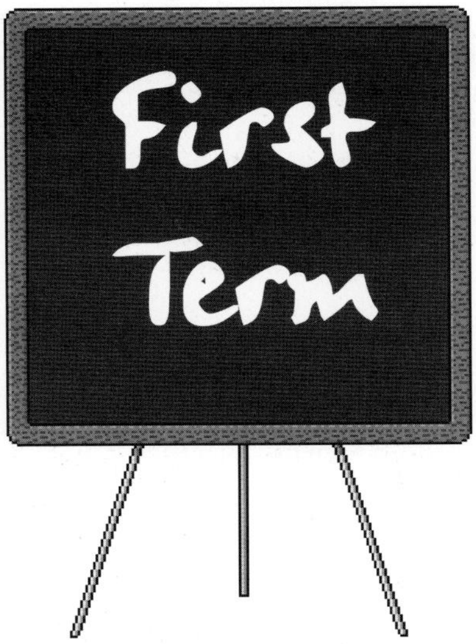

Introduce the idea to teacher colleagues to gain their support. Suggest that groups of teachers and parents might work together to produce tailor-made materials for the school eg Early Years teachers and parents could develop further information sheets for history orientated story books. Middle Years teachers and parents might produce further buildings leaflets linked more specifically to buildings in the neighbourhood of the school.

Seek support of parent volunteers (ensuring that parents who are otherwise teachers or professional historians do not dominate the groups).

Inform Governors of plans.

Parent/teacher groups to meet as appropriate. Enlist support of Schools Library Service (to provide examples of books) and people with local knowledge of buildings, as required.

Class teachers to begin to collect together children's work which demonstrates the *History at Home* skills in action.

For example, this might include work resulting from:

■ visits to interesting buildings showing the children investigating the evidence through observing, questioning and deducing

■ using artefacts, either in school or at museums, and demonstrating similar skills as above

■ talking to elderly people and looking at photographs and pictures

■ the reading of stories with a history focus

■ developing children's understanding of sequence and chronology through time lines

■ any of the above which show how learning in history develops skills across the curriculum.

Parent/teacher groups to continue

Peter Hollinshead

High rise blocks can be found in most large towns and cities.

to meet as necessary to work towards finished products for distribution.

Class teachers to continue to collect childrens' work.

Arrange a history event towards the end of the term.

When designing the event:

■ involve the parent helpers/Parents Association/teacher colleagues on the steering group.

■ encourage the parent helpers to take part in the event - their support will be vital in persuading other parents that *History at Home* is worth becoming involved in.

■ involve children in the event (a bigger audience will result!). It is a good occasion to promote the school, explain to parents what history at school is all about, and the children themselves can demonstrate how the skills and concepts which will be developed by *History at Home* will help their work in school.

■ consider gathering as many resources together as possible, to give parents further ideas of what constitutes history.

The event should:

■ provide parents with information about the nature and content of the History National Curriculum.

■ demonstrate the relevance of *History at Home* to school work.

■ pass on to parents questioning techniques used by teachers to help children investigate.

Encourage parents that this is something they can do.

Raise parents' confidence by giving them a number of handouts to take home, both those created by the school and photocopies of appropriate ones in this book.

Show families doing *History at Home* activities in the English Heritage video *'History at Home'*, presented by David Bellamy.

■ indicate that there is no expectation that every family will involve themselves in all aspects of *History at Home*. Point out that families can take advantage of opportunities as they arise, and that one visit, story or conversation is unlikely to exhaust all the possibilities, as everyone will become better investigators with practice.

■ give everyone an enjoyable evening where history is shown to be fun.

It is very important that the school helps to maintain the enthusiasm engendered by the launching event. This can be done by:

■ ensuring that each class is involved in some history work during the following term, so that links between *History at Home* and schoolwork become explicit.

■ encouraging children, who have been following *History at Home* activities, to talk about what they have done to the rest of the class. This could be complemented by asking them to add information to the class time line and providing a display space for history items that have emerged through home activities. Some of this could be done during assemblies when parents are present, or by mounting a display in the entrance area or another location where parents would have access to.

■ considering the development of a book loan scheme (possibly run by the parents) where the history story books can be borrowed and exchanged on a regular basis.

■ remembering to involve parents of children new to the school in the scheme.

A two term lead-in will ensure that there is enough time to prepare for the event without losing the momentum resulting from initial enthusiasm. It is a good policy to have the event shortly before a holiday period, as it is during holidays that families will be more likely to have opportunities for taking part in *History at Home* activities. The period before Easter is probably the best time as it allows the school to maintain the impetus during the summer term. Although the summer holiday may provide parents with more opportunities, the hiatus caused by the long holiday and the start of the new school year in September does not make it as easy for the school to ensure continuity.

Peter Hollinshead

Using the home as a starting point will involve investigating all forms of housing, high rise blocks, houses divided into flats, houses, bungalows, cottages, chalets and mobile homes. This townscape would allow discussion about the features of the older terraced houses and how they have been modified, and comparisons could be made about different housing styles.

HISTORY AT HOME ACROSS THE CURRICULUM

Mike Corbishley

Children investigating their local historic environment.

English Heritage

Using different measuring equipment.

The *History at Home* project does not only develop historical skills, concepts and knowledge. The sources of historical evidence will also allow children to increase their knowledge and skills in most of the other subjects of the curriculum.

DESIGN AND TECHNOLOGY

Two areas of home-based investigations in particular will make a contribution to children's understanding of design and technology. First, the emphasis on historical artefacts will provide opportunities to consider the materials that were used, and how and why they have changed. Second, the study of a variety of old buildings will allow consideration of a range of building materials and the factors that influenced people's decision as to what to use. In addition it will become apparent that changing needs resulted in different designs, for example railway stations modelled on traditional building styles.

MATHS

Buildings provide a variety of opportunities to develop concepts associated with shape, and to use the language of mathematics. Facades of houses are composed of a variety of shapes, and those of churches often contain more complex patterns. The older the house, the greater the patterning. 'Black and White' houses incorporate a huge range of patterns on their facades. Victorian houses often include tessellations in the form of tiling. Medieval and Tudor buildings sometimes contain patterned ceilings and some very interesting patterns in the shapes of the leaded window panes. At home, artefacts can be sorted in a variety of ways, for example old and new, or by material.

ENGLISH

It would be impossible for families to become involved with *History at Home* without developing children's English skills. Speaking and listening skills will be enhanced in every context:

- speaking to and listening to relatives
- having a discussion about an artefact at home or in a museum
- investigating an old building
- listening to a story being read.

In addition there are many opportunities for children to practise reading, whether it be reading parts of a guidebook or labels in a museum, or reading a story for themselves. Some simple family documents may involve the challenge of reading styles of handwriting that have gone out of fashion.

English Heritage

RIGHT: Industrial museums can be a good source of examples of early technology.

Key Stage 1 children recording data for a science project.

Art activity at Kenilworth Castle.

Geography at an historic site.

SCIENCE

The method of enquiry involved in science has similarities to that in history. The asking of questions, hypothesizing and the collection of evidence to test the hypothesis (with the idea of a fair test) is as appropriate to history as to science. For example the question 'are old gravestones always more eroded?' can be answered through approaching the evidence in a systematic way.

Some of the *History at Home* activities will also allow children to discover a world without some of the results of scientific discovery which we take for granted - a world without electricity or the internal combustion engine.

ART

Much of the evidence for the past is the product of the work of artists, craftspeople and photographers. Through looking at artefacts, whether they be decorative or practical, and by observation of portraits and other paintings, prints and drawings, children are not only looking at a source of evidence for the past, but gaining an understanding of artistic traditions and inspiration for their own creative work. The nature of photographs and the work of photographers should not be forgotten.

GEOGRAPHY

Geographical skills and knowledge will be enhanced through the buildings section of *History at Home*. Buildings studied in the home area will help develop the child's sense of place. Buildings looked at on holiday or visiting relatives elsewhere will enhance the understanding of a distant, and therefore, different place. If the children work out the routes that are to be taken when walking around the local community, or visiting a place further afield, then their mapwork skills will develop. Any discussion of issues about why old buildings are preserved, will introduce the idea that choices are available to society.

RELIGIOUS EDUCATION

Knowledge of, and the appreciation of the value to society of, places of worship, will be developed through visiting both local examples, and places of national importance. Talking with elderly people will encourage relationships and the valuing of other people's contributions to society.

ENVIRONMENTAL AWARENESS

The built environment is often given a lower profile than the natural environment. Any work on buildings which results from *History at Home* will help to redress this balance, while at the same time highlighting the variety, history and aesthetic appeal of both individual, and groups of, buildings.

MULTI-CULTURAL EDUCATION

The changing use, and occupancy of buildings, especially in some urban areas, reflects the multi-ethnic nature of British society. Even buildings, such as stately homes, which appear to be archetypically British will, on closer examination, reveal architectural influences from elsewhere (eg Greece and Italy) and may include, among their contents, examples of furniture and artefacts from many countries around the world. The inspiration for, and interior decoration of, many British buildings, is an amalgam of cultural influences from around the world.

Investigating the natural environment around a ruined building.

BIBLIOGRAPHY AND RESOURCES

BOOKS TO READ WITH YOUNGER CHILDREN

Ahlberg, J & A, **Peepo**, Penguin (Picture Puffin), 1983. ISBN 0-14050-384-6. Domestic scenes of the 1940s seen through the eyes of the baby.

Dupasquier,P, **Our House on the Hill**, Anderson Press, 1988. ISBN 0-86264-167-5. A book that provides a month by month account of a comfortable, happy, often familiar, family life over the period of a year.

Fox, M, **Wilfred Gordon McDonald Partridge**, Penguin (Picture Puffin), 1987. ISBN 0-14050-586-5. A story about the relationship between a child and elderly people. Wilfred does not see them as old.

Ives, P, **Granny's Quilt**, Hamilton, 1993. ISBN 0-24113-274-6. Granny's life story is revealed as she talks about her quilt, made of scraps of fabric from clothes she once wore.

Rogers, E and P, **Our House**, Walker, 1992. ISBN 0-7445-2022-3. The story of a house and its occupants from the 1780s to the 1990s.

Rogers, P, **From Me to You**, Orchard, 1987. ISBN 1-85213-060-1. A simple story told by Grandma linking an Edwardian childhood through the Second World War to the present day.

Waddell, M, **Grandma's Bill**, Simon and Schuster, 1991. ISBN 0-75000-307-3. A story of a grandma sharing memories with her grandson of the granddad he never knew, through the family photograph album.

Waddell, M, **Once There Were Giants**, Walker, 1991. ISBN 0-7445-1791-5. A beautifully illustrated story of a baby growing up amongst "giants", her mother, father and uncle Tom, until she eventually marries and has her own baby.

Waddell, M, **The Hidden House**, Walker, 1992. ISBN 0-7445-1797-4. A man makes some dolls for company, leaving them in the house when he leaves.

Waddell, M, **The Toymaker**, Walker, 1993. ISBN 0-7445-3018-0. A story in two parts. A toymaker makes dolls for his daughter back in the nineteenth century. A modern child descendant of the toymaker visits the now empty shop with her grandmother.

Walsh, J Paton, **Thomas and the Tinners**, Macdonald, 1995. ISBN 0-75001-533-0. An award-winning story set in the industrial landscape of the tin mines.

Williams, M, **When I Was Little**, Walker, 1991. ISBN 0-7445-1765-6. In strip format a grandparent recalls the differences between her childhood and her grandchild's life.

Zolotow, C, **This Quiet Lady**, Greenwillow Books, 1992. ISBN 0-688-09305-1. A mother and child reminisce about the past in comparison to the present.

STORIES FOR OLDER CHILDREN

Avery, G, **Mouldy's Orphan**, Penguin (Puffin), 1981. ISBN 0-14031-269-2. Set in the Victorian countryside, the story revolves around Mouldy's attempt to adopt a poor orphan boy.

Davis, E, **Clues in the Desert**, Mantra, 1983. ISBN 1-85269-097-6. Asif investigates the remains of the Indus Valley civilisation with his archaeologist aunt.

Foreman, M, **The Boy Who Sailed with Columbus**, Pavilion, 1992. ISBN 1-85145-803-4. A beautifully illustrated story of a cabin boy who sailed with Columbus on his first voyage and stayed in the West Indies living with the indigenous people until the Spaniards returned.

Foreman, M, **War Boy**, Pavilion Books, 1989. ISBN 1-85145-353-9; and **After the war was over**, Pavilion Books, 1995. ISBN 1-85793-553-5. These two beautifully illustrated and written books tell of the author's own life during the Second World War and immediately afterwards.

Garfield, L, **Smith**, Penguin (Puffin), 1970. ISBN 0-14030-349-9. A fast moving story about a young urchin in eighteenth-century London.

Gerrard, R. **Sir Cedric**, Gollancz, 1985. ISBN 0-57504-334-2. A story told in rhyming verse of knights of old, in which Sir Cedric rescues the Lady Matilda from Black Ned.

Innocenti, R, (illustrated) **Rose Blanche**, Cape, 1985. ISBN 0-22402-841-3. An eloquent and haunting picture book highlighting a child's experience of war.

Jones, T, **The Saga of Erik the Viking**, Penguin (Puffin), 1988. ISBN 0-14032-261-2. Adventures from Viking times in saga style. Beautifully illustrated.

Lattimore, DN, **The Winged Cat**, a tale of ancient Egypt, Harper Collins, 1992. ISBN 0-06023-635-3. In this realistically illustrated text, a servant girl's quest for justice takes her through the gates of the Netherworld.

Lively, P, **The Ghost of Thomas Kempe**, Mammoth, 1992. ISBN 0-74970-791-7. James finds himself in a seventeenth-century cottage which had been occupied by a sorcerer.

Mathews, S S, **The Sad Night: the story of an Aztec victory and a Spanish loss**, Clarion, 1994. ISBN 0-39563-035-5. A magnificently illustrated book of some of the events of the Spanish conquest of the Aztecs, written from the Aztec point of view.

McCaughrean, G, **The Orchard Book of Greek Myths**, Orchard, 1992. ISBN 1-85213-373-2. A retelling of sixteen well known myths.

Magorian, M, **Goodnight Mister Tom**, Penguin (Puffin), 1983. ISBN 0-14031-541-1. A London child is evacuated to the country where all goes well until he receives a summons from his mother to return home.

Paton Walsh, J, **Lost and Found**, Deutsch, 1984. ISBN 0-23397-

672-8. Four episodes in which a household item is lost by a child and found by a later generation.

Sutcliff, R, **Black Ships Before Troy**, F Lincoln, 1993. ISBN 0-71120-778-X. A modern well illustrated re-telling of The Iliad, which includes the famous stories connected with the wooden horse at the seige of Troy.

Paton Walsh, J, and French, F, **Pepi and the Secret Names**, Frances Lincoln, 1994. ISBN 0-7112-0867-0. A story set in Ancient Egypt which requires hieroglyphics to be deciphered.

Wild, M, **Let the Celebrations Begin**, Bodley Head, 1991. ISBN 0-37031-605-3. A picture book which depicts life in a concentration camp and the joy of release and freedom. It is recommended that adults should read it through first.

BOOKS FOR CHILDREN

About artefacts

Bryant-Mole, K, **History from Objects: In the Home**, Wayland, 1993. ISBN 0-7502-1017-6.

Tanner, G, and Wood, T, **History Mysteries: Cleaning**, A & C Black, 1994. ISBN 0-7136-3802-8.

Thompson, R, **Changing Times: Cooking,** Franklin Watts, 1992. ISBN 0-7496-0891-9.

Thompson, R, **Changing Times: Toys and Games**, Franklin Watts, 1992. ISBN 0-7496-0873-0.

About religious buildings

Gandiol-Coppin, B, **The Building of the Great Cathedrals**, Moonlight Publishing, 1988. ISBN 1-85103-042-5

Macaulay, D, **Cathedral: the story of its construction**, William Collins, 1974. ISBN 0-00-1921509.

Macdonld, F and Bergin, M, **A Sixteenth-Century Mosque**, Simon and Schuster, 1994. ISBN 0-7500-1414-8

Macdonald, F and James, J, A **Medieval Cathedral**, Simon and Schuster, 1991. ISBN 0-7500-0787-7.

About homes

Barden, H, **Houses and Homes**, Wayland, 1994. ISBN 0-7502-0331-5.

MacDonald, F, **Timelines: Houses**, Franklin Watts, 1994. ISBN 0-7496-1538-9.

Ross, S, **Starting History: Where We Lived**, Wayland, 1994. ISBN 0-7502-1360-4.

Wood, R, **Tudors and Stuarts Homes**, Wayland, 1994. ISBN 0-7502-1152-0.

About railways

Wood, S, **Trains and Railways**, Dorling Kindersley, 1992. ISBN 0-86318-815-X.

Macdonald, F, **A Nineteenth-Century Railway Station**, Simon and Schuster, 1990. ISBN 0-7500-0215-8.

About shops

Cooke, J, **Shops**, Wayland, 1986. ISBN 0-85078-625-8.

Ross, S, **Starting History: Shopping**, Wayland, 1992. ISBN 0-7502-0333-1.

Tanner, G, and Wood, T, **History Mysteries: Shopping**, A & C Black, 1992. ISBN 0-7136-3689-0.

Thompson, R, **Shopping for Food**, Franklin Watts, 1992. ISBN 0-7596-0895-0.

BOOKS FOR PARENTS AND TEACHERS

About buildings

Gray, E, **The British House: A Concise Architectural History**, Barrie and Jenkins, 1994. ISBN 0-7126-6589-6.

Iredale, D, **Discovering Your Old House,** Shire, 1991. ISBN 0-7478-0143-6.

Jenner, M, **The Architectural Heritage of Britain and Ireland**, Michael Joseph, 1993. ISBN 0-7181-3517-2.

West, TW, **Discovering English Architecture**, Shire, 1979. ISBN 0-85263-455-2.

About churches

Child, M, **Discovering Church Architecture**, Shire, 1991. ISBN 0-85263-328-9.

Clowney P & T, **Exploring Churches**, Lion, 1993. ISBN 0-7459-2771-8.

Cunnington, P, **How Old Is That Church?**, Marston House, 1993. ISBN 0-9517700-9-8.

About country houses

Girouard, M, **Life in the English Country House: A Social and Architectural History**, Yale, 1978. ISBN 0-300-02273-5.

About families

Iredale, D, **Your Family Tree: A Handbook on Tracing Ancestors and Compiling One's Own Pedigree**, Shire, 1985. ISBN 0-85263-767-5.

About museums

Barton, KJ, **Southern England and the Channel Islands**, HMSO, 1992. ISBN 0-11-290468-8.

Hatton, A, **East Anglia**, HMSO, 1992. ISBN 0-11-290472-6.

Fleming, D, **North East England**, HMSO, 1989. ISBN 0-11-290470-X.

Jenkins, G, **Wales**, HMSO, 1990. ISBN 0-11-290467-X.

Marsh, G, Hoare, N and Hull, K, **The Home Counties**, HMSO, 1990. ISBN 0-11-290471-8.

Olding, S, **South West England**, HMSO, 1989. ISBN 0-11-290469-6.

Phillips, D, **North West England and the Isle of Man**, HMSO, 1989. ISBN 0-11-290473-4.

Popplewell, S, **Ireland**, HMSO, 1990. ISBN 0-11-290475-0.

Schadla-Hall, T, **The Midlands**, HMSO, 1992. ISBN 0-11-290466-1.

Thompson, C, **Scotland**, HMSO, 1990. ISBN 0-11-290474-2.

Wilson, A, **South West England**, HMSO, 1989. ISBN 0-11-290469-6.

About railways

Cockman, FG, **Railway Architecture**, Shire, 1988. ISBN 0-85263-917-1.

FAMILY DISCOVERY PACKS

Written primarily for family groups, these packs English Heritage would be a useful resource for teachers planning a site visit. Each contains two activity cards encouraging observational skills and a wallchart with practical ideas to use in the classroom.

Audley End,
ISBN 1-85074-218-9
Battle Abbey and The Battle of Hastings, *ISBN 1-85074-267-7*
Clifford's Tower and York city walls, *ISBN 1-85074-324-X*
Kenilworth Castle,
ISBN 1-85074-294-4
Rievaulx Abbey,
ISBN 1-85074-171-1
Tintagel Castle,
ISBN 1-85074-322-3
Totnes Castle,
ISBN 1-85074-284-7

CHILDREN'S ACTIVITY BOOKS

Some English Heritage sites which are open to the public have activity guides written especially for Key Stage 2 children.These books contain a number of interesting activities which might help parents and teachers devise *History at Home* projects for historic sites in their own area.

Dover Castle,
ISBN 1-85074-504-8
Framlingham and Orford Castles, ISBN 1-85074-505-6
Hadrian's Wall,
ISBN 1-85074-503-X
Whitby Abbey,
ISBN 1-85074-506-4

EDUCATIONAL APPROACHES

Education on Site is a series of English Heritage teacher's guides which suggest educational strategies for using the historic environment as part of National Curriculum work.

Alderton, D, **Using industrial sites**, English Heritage, 1995. ISBN 1-85074-445-9.

Barnicoat, J, **Newspapers and conservation**, English Heritage, 1994. ISBN 1-85074-511-0.

Copeland, T, **Using castles**, English Heritage, 1993. ISBN 1-85074-327-4.

Copeland, T, **Geography and the historic environment**, English Heritage, 1993. ISBN 1-85074-332-0.

Copeland, T, **Maths and the historic environment**, English Heritage, 1992. ISBN 1-85074-329-0.

Durbin, G, **Using historic houses**, English Heritage, 1993. ISBN 1-85074-390-8.

Durbin, G, Morris, S & Wilkinson, S, **Learning from objects**, English Heritage, 1990. ISBN 1-85074-259-6.

Fairclough,J, **History through role play**, English Heritage, 1994. ISBN 1-85074-478-5.

Keith, C, **Using listed buildings**, English Heritage, 1991. ISBN 1-85074-297-9.

Maddern, E, **Storytelling at historic sites**, English Heritage, 1992. ISBN 1-85074-378-9.

Pownall, J & Hutson, **Science and the historic environment**, English Heritage, 1992. ISBN 1-85074-331-2.

Purkis, S, **Using memorials**, English Heritage, 1995. ISBN 1-85074-493-9.

Purkis, S, **Using school buildings**, English Heritage, 1993. ISBN 1-85074-379-7.

VIDEOS

The archaeological detectives, 1990/91, 79 minutes, English Heritage. Four videos which show teams of children discover evidence for themselves in buildings and artefacts.

Teaching on site: National Curriculum subjects and the historic environment, 1991/92, 73 minutes, English Heritage. In-service and ITT.

History at Home, 1994, 23 minutes, English Heritage. *The History at Home* project involving two families, their schools, presented by David Bellamy.

AUDIO

Storytelling at historic sites - a selection of myths, legends and folktales for Britain told by Eric Maddern, 2x90 min. cassettes; 1992

Acknowledgements

The author would like to thank the following for their help during the project: Parents and teachers from the Cumbrian primary schools of Gilsland; Hallbankgate; St Thomas', Kendal; Long Marton; St Mark's, Natland; Orton; Roose; Sedbergh; Beaconside Infant School, Penrith. Nicola Hunter (Cumbria Schools Library Service), June Hall (Abbot Hall Museum and Art Gallery, Kendal), Susan Dench (Cumbria Archives Service), Philippa Hope (Lancaster University Library) and family, Jo Jackson and family, Cherry Trelogan and family, Paul and Monica Kimche and family, Geoff Brambles for the original drawings for the buildings leaflets and Liz Clement for their design. Hilary Cooper, Pam Tipping, Christine Burgess and Mike Huggins for reading and commenting on the manuscript; Margaret Hartley for typing the manuscript; the Trustees of Abbot Hall Art Gallery, Kendal and the owners of a number of shops in Ambleside for permission to photograph.

The editor would like to thank the Anderson Press, the Orchard Press, Mantra Publishing and Victor Gollancz for allowing reproduction of the books on pages 12-13.

OPPOSITE PAGE: Family photographs (English Heritage).

Our Education Service aims to help teachers at all levels make better use of the resource of the historic environment. Educational groups can make free visits to over 400 historic properties cared for by English Heritage. The following booklets are free on request. **Free Educational Visits, Using the Historic Environment**. Our **Resources** catalogue is also available. Please contact:

English Heritage
Education Service
429 Oxford Street
London
W1R 2HD

Tel: 0171 973 3442
Fax: 0171 973 3443